Curses
for
Every Occasion

By Tracey Curtis
and Robert Goller

Beaten Track
www.beatentrackpublishing.com

Curses for Every Occasion

Published 2019 by Beaten Track Publishing
Copyright © 2019 Tracey Curtis and Robert Goller

ISBN:
978 1 78645 305 1 (Paperback)
978 1 78645 306 8 (eBook)

Beaten Track Publishing,
Burscough. Lancashire.
www.beatentrackpublishing.com

Foreword

I've known Tracey for a couple of decades now, and it probably won't surprise you to know – given the content of this book – that over that time, I've come to both expect and enjoy her biting, potty-mouthed cynicism, invariably defending myself against her timely, withering put-downs.

Actually, that's all a lie – in all the time I've known Tracey, I've found her to be unnerringly polite and well-mannered, so this book of blistering insults at first seemed wholly out of character. But then again...

Insults, especially when they're devastatingly, bitingly funny, are perfect for those of us whose preferred mode of attack isn't to roll up our sleeves and punch someone in the face. My mum once told me (probably paraphrasing many other mums down the years) that 'if you resort to swearing then you've lost the argument'. Swearing, like punching, is too easy, too obvious, a fool's way out. Insults, however – they're a surprise package, and they come with a stickiness that's hard to forget. By using the silliest wordsmithery, you disarm and disconcert your opponent.

I can imagine the expression on the face of the bully who is told 'May the letterbox rattle when you're on the toilet'. I can picture the expression of utter puzzlement when you warn that sneering office co-worker 'may you accidentally get your skirt caught on the office printer and reveal your Friday pants on a Tuesday'.

Having the perfect (and perfectly absurd) put-down ready for all life's circumstances isn't easy, and that's why this book of curses can be your handy guide into the exciting world of barbed one-liners. What makes it all the more useful is its simple categorisation – who would have imagined that there would be a specific set of curses for, say, an overbearing theatrical friend? (Even the most committed thespian would struggle to recover from 'May Pam Ayres appear in your room, moments before going on stage'.)

Among the qualities of a good (and effective) curse, one of the most striking is absurdity. This book manages to cleverly turn rage into Dada poetry, making the insult not only funny but utterly surreal. I am still trying to fathom the ludicrous beauty of 'May you pronounce the word "Lego" wrongly when purchasing some for your nephew'.

I'm still trying to fathom half of the curses in this collection. Like I said, these curses – they come with a stickiness that's hard to forget.

Boff Whalley (Chumbawamba)

Introduction

Curses have been in use for millions of years. Since dinosaurs developed vocal cords, in fact, hence the well-known curse: *'May you lay three hundred eggs and forget where the father lives!'* and *'May you end up in the Museum of Natural History!'*

Nowadays, curses are just as venomous but a little more appropriate to twenty-first-century living.

If used properly, these curses can prevent you from becoming hotheaded and resorting to violence when in stressful situations. Just breathe deeply, calmly get out your pocket book of curses and deliver the appropriate curse.

Please bear in mind that these curses are extremely potent when delivered with the correct gaze and voice* (this should come easily with practice), so remember – only use them in necessary situations and not just because you don't like a person or because they smell of Intimately Beckham.

Curse wisely!

* To use one of these curses, you must follow these three steps:

1.   Narrow your eyes.

2.   Point to the cursee.

3.   Deliver the curse from the back of the throat, in a growl (think Linda Blair playing Regan MacNeil in *The Exorcist*).

Or you can just post/email/text the curse.

Index

Vanity

May you be wearing your worst pair
of pants when the vicar comes for tea.

May your best hat get crumpled
on the number 49 bus.

May you find your left eyebrow
deeply embarrassing.

May your best foot smell
and get bunions.

May your next perm
go horribly wrong.

May your middle name be Maud.

May you have a snot bubble when you
next talk to the vicar.

May you breathe pickled onions at the dentist.

May you sneeze out
a pea at Sunday lunch.

May your well-known 'plum pud' go disastrously
wrong at the church fête.

May your anus feel damp and sticky for
all the time you're at a neighbour's barbecue,
but be curiously dry when you check
it on arriving home.

May all your shoes be brown.

May you mistake your reading glasses for a
spoon whilst on a date, realise your error but,
to save face, pretend not to notice and eat
a whole bowlful of lentil soup with them.

May you buy a skirt that goes with nothing.

May a hard, greenish-black, crispy bogey
fall out of your nose in a silent corridor.

May you demand a facial skin graft
from your bottom for your sun-damaged skin
and be devastated to find a hairy anus,
just under your right eye,
on waking up post-surgery.

May your shower cap have perforations.

May your longest fingernail break
at a jewellery party.

May your right leg spasm on the catwalk.

May your toupée slip forward at
a meringue-eating contest.

May your tongue be furry on a first date.

May your favourite perfume become Old Spice.

May your favourite cardigan
unravel on a tent peg.

May you make excuses for your burnt Soufflé
with three yards of lead pipe poking
out of your left nostril.

May your dog like your sister more than you.

May your armpits squelch and
your teeth become asymmetrical.

May all your clothes become
three sizes too small.

May you discover three hairy moles
on your recently extracted wisdom tooth.

May your breath come out brown
on a cold winter morning.

May your husband's squash partner
tell you he finds you physically repulsive.

May your dandruff be as large
as a dolphin during the FA Cup Final.

May you fart out of your mouth
whilst discussing an overdraft
with your bank manager.

May you see your reflection
as a strawberry and nut sundae
with extra chocolate sauce,
for a month.

May your bum cleavage spread
to the back of your neck
for half an hour during
Take the High Road
on Wednesday afternoon.

May you mistake your mascara for
lipstick for four months before noticing.

May you accidentally wear
your wife's crotchless knickers
at the swimming club.

May you remember
the best night
of your life
accurately
(involving sex,
moderate fame
and an all-night party)
but when telling people,
be unable
to stop yourself
describing
an intense game
of table tennis
in
all
its
intricate
detail.

Snobbery

May your washing
not come out bluey-white.

May your sister-in-law spill tea
on your best tablecloth.

May your favourite pot plant
get too much sunlight.

May your toaster jam up
and your kettle fur.

May you have to open
your pedal-bin manually.

May your neighbour's cat
dig up your lupins.

May your friends
laugh at your cutlery.

May your furry toilet seat
develop mildew.

May your bluebells be yellow.

May your favourite dog
turn into a shit.

May your friends find out you buy
Happy Shopper tea.

May your living room colour scheme
be lime green and beige.

May your fridge magnets
lose their magnetism
and your oven door squeak.

May your peaceful cottage in Devon
turn into the Exeter Corn Exchange.

May your neighbour borrow your new lawn
mower and give you an old one back.

May your best china
be mysteriously misplaced
on the compost heap.

May your hot chocolate
taste of garlic for a week.

May all your desserts
taste of cabbage.

May you name your new house
Keith and Angie's Doll's House.

May you turn up at
a party with
the same dress
as the vicar's wife.

May you find out all of your friends
have been calling you Big Blood.

May your pony shit on

The Duchess of Cambridge's shoe

at the local gymkhana.

May your curtains fade

and your lampshade wither.

May you be pleasantly surprised

by doing a poo in your bidet

and tell all your friends about it.

May you find your

favourite earrings

in a Christmas cracker.

May you find your

favourite dishwasher

in a Christmas cracker.

Utter Rudeness

May your husband's moustache
get burnt off
in a fire-eating contest.

May you sit on a cupcake
and be mortified.

May your toenails
dissolve in the bath.

May your daughter lose
her next tennis match.

May your foot feel
uncomfortable by the poolside.

May the ghost of Sigmund Freud sit
opposite you, smirking, whenever you're
in conversation with your mother.

May you find yourself
under someone's
sweaty armpit on the Tube
from Waterloo to High Barnet.

May your bum cheeks
stick together
when you next
meet the vicar.

May your son's satchel smell
of egg mayonnaise.

May the letterbox rattle
when you're on the toilet.

May a candelabra
appear in your bathroom.

May you dream
of pickled eggs
all next summer.

May you turn into Bert Reynolds
at your son's parents' evening.

May you call
your firstborn
Florida-Anne.

May it rain on every barbecue
you hold for the next four years.

May your sphincter whistle
'Colonel Bogey' in public.

May your record collection
be disappointing on Tuesday.

May your son turn into Big Ron
at your Tupperware party.

May your husband
take up the accordion.

May your granny
step in the litter tray.

May your stomach rumble loudly
during an embarrassing silence.

May your granny want to talk about
her friend, Mrs Steele, all day on Sunday.

May some earwax fall
onto your job application form.

May your dog have a phantom pregnancy.

May the taste of rancid broccoli
remind you of your first kiss.

May your daughter have forty-six ugly
boyfriends before she settles down to marry.

May your seat be
facing the wall at the cinema.

May your daughter call you a 'fat halibut'
at the doctor's surgery.

May your doorbell be
permanently pressed in.

May your bathroom
turn into a mobile library.

May you think your toilet paper
is an infectious disease
and be terrified.

May you be desperate for a poo
during choir practice.

May your favourite television show
be *Busman's Holiday*.

May you read a book with
the last page missing.

May your doctor call you 'Celia' for a laugh.

May you be instantly scared
of birds in an aviary.

May you be wary of crocuses
and daffodils all next spring.

May your piles flare up
in a cushion testing factory.

May you be wedged
between two sumo wrestlers
and a crate of Earl Grey tea.

May you lose three consecutive games
of chess to your husband's best friend.

May your firstborn be possessed with
a 'cut here' tattoo on her umbilical cord.

May your son buy
a Celine Dion album
and play it constantly
for two weeks.

May your bowels not be
as regular as they once were.

May your ears pop during
the school's rendition of
*Joseph and the Amazing
Technicolour Dreamcoat*.

May your cat
give birth to kittens
on your hairdressing folder.

May your husband accidentally
put your new shelves up
in your neighbour's house.

May you develop a craving for
crème brûlée de poils pubiens,
during pregnancy.

May Andre Previn engrave

a limerick on your front door

for a laugh.

May you dream you are entering
the Tour de France and be
bitterly disappointed on awakening.

May your pants fall down during
the parents' three-legged race
at your son's school sports day.

May you find yourself singing
'Tutti zitti'
from *Madame Butterfly*,
at your local pub.

May you fall in love
with a wandering minstrel.

May all your chat-up lines
come out in
a Pauline Fowler voice.

May your husband turn into
Ken Dodd for three days.

May you always imagine your partner
to be a French bulldog when having sex.

May your thoughts be visible
in the dentist's waiting room.

May your husband take to wearing
burgundy felt slippers
with seams up the middle.

May your regular church group vanish.

May your Aunt Edwina smoke
those awful cigars
in your living room on Sunday.

May all your friends be called
Nicholas Parsons
for the next ten years.

May you be unable to flush away
a huge poo at the vicarage.

May you be grounded for
nine years for washing
your mum's best nightdress
in bleach.

May you find an ageing falafel
in the cupboard under the sink.

May you wake up one morning
with cornflakes between your toes.

May you discover that you had
rheumatic fever twice as a child.

May you be doing the vacuuming nude
and slip up and land on a mango.

May you find yourself petrified
of water in a Jacuzzi.

May you sprain your ankle
on your daughter's roller skate
and get no sympathy.

May your daughter see your
pyloric sphincter and laugh.

May you find yourself stuck
with the letters XXYVWPT
when playing Scrabble.

May you find yourself striving
to do The Conga with everyone
in the high street on Saturday.

May you be unable
to spot your own son
in his annual class photo.

May your favourite James Bond film
be a figment of your imagination.

May you find yourself
regularly approaching
your friend's pet gerbil
for sound financial advice.

Greed

May your best silverware
be melted down in
a supervised fireworks display.

May all your credentials
fall into a tube
of liquid nitrogen.

May you find
something 'orrible
in a Spud-U-Like potato.

May you find Brussels sprout pie
seasoned with cinnamon
to be the only item on every menu
in town on Friday night.

May you think your loofah
is a baguette and eat it.

May your friend take
a handful of crisps
when you offer him only one.

May you overbid at an auction.

May there be two feathers
on your lemon drizzle cake.

May you, when offered a choice
between after-dinner mints
and coffee creams,
be unable to decide
and have neither.

May all the crosses turn into
noughts on your hot-cross buns.

May you be unable to find
your favourite coffee flavour
in a packet of Starbursts.

May your mother eat all the vowels
in your Scrabble game.

May your stairs and landing
need re-carpeting at
a very bad financial time.

May you only inherit
a tin of sliced peaches
in syrup from
your favourite uncle's estate.

May you find you like your
favourite meal less and less.

May you overspend on
joke sweets and whoopie cushions.

May you leave all your
Easter eggs by the radiator.

May three men with kind smiles
befriend your grandmother,
only to steal her lucky bingo pants.

May your muffins land
butter side down
for a period of
not less than two years.

May you put all your money
on a blind, arthritic horse called
'You Must be Fucking Joking, Right?'

Driving

May you fail your driving test for insisting on
showing your examiner your new home.

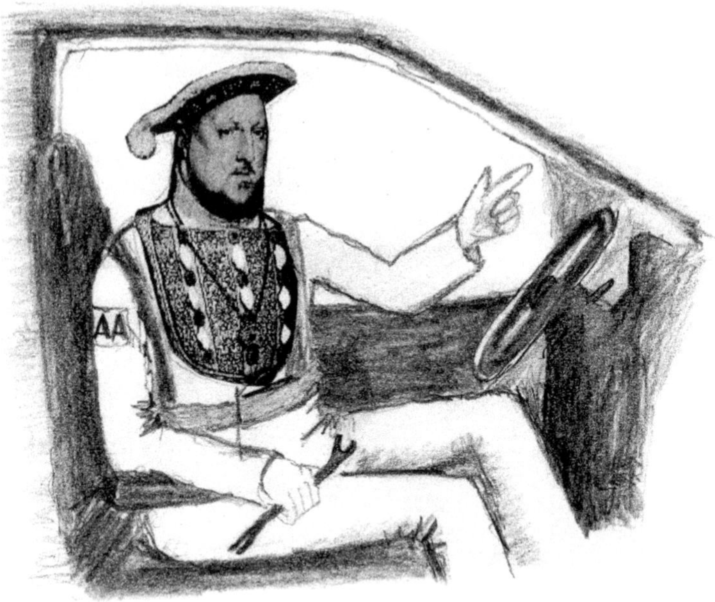
AA

May the AA man leave oily fingerprints on your dashboard whilst trying to do an impersonation of King Henry VIII.

May you stick to the car seat
whilst driving home from the beach.

May you fail your driving test
for calling your examiner 'Cod Lips'.

May the woodwind section of the Swindon
Symphony Orchestra, and all their dogs,
be parked outside your garage
when you return home from work.

May your driving instructor
turn into a huge
blackberry and apple turnover
just as you approach
your first set of traffic lights.

May your tyres be square.

The Arts

May you agree to illustrate a book
for a friend, be unable to admit that
you can't draw and,
rather than face the music,
deliberately dismantle your arms
as though they were made of Lego.

May all your paints harden on your palette.

May your life model turn into a bowl of fruit
halfway through your A Level art exam.

May the lanky, ginger one from
The Full Monty be sitting in front
of your shortest relative at the
premiere screening of your new arty film.

May your art lecturer devour your
still life while you're on your tea break.

May your creative days
always be a washout.

May all your paintbrushes
become toothbrushes
yet you still
have to have fillings.

May you tell all your friends the title
of your new novel *The Devil Liketh Thee*
but be unable to write anything other than...

One day there was a little girl who went

on an adventure and then she woke up

and it had all been a dream.

May you mistake your piano for your
guitar and get into all sorts of trouble
on the train to your next gig.

May everything you paint look
suspiciously like a saucy postcard.

May you finally get to meet your favourite author at a book signing, but the conversation between you go like this:

"Hi!"

"What?"

"Hi!"

"What?"

"Nothing."

"What?"

"Nothing!"

"You said what?"

"I said 'Hi'!"

"What?"

"I said 'Hi' before."

"You said 'Nothing' before!"

"I said 'Hi'!"

"You said you said 'Nothing'!"

"Hi, then."

"What?"

"Oh, for fuck's sake!"

"How dare you talk to me like that at my own book signing! Get out of here!"

May you be plagued

by pretentious arty types

in all your dreams

for a month.

May your art teacher tell you

you're going to become

a well-respected and successful artist

and then take the piss out of you

to his colleagues.

May the only person

willing to write

a foreword for

your new book be

a member of the defunct,

one-hit-wonder band,

Chumbawamba.

Work

May you find yourself accidentally fondling

your business partner's pencil case.

May you discover you're the most boring
person in the office this year.

May you accidentally call your boss
'Cuddles' at your annual appraisal.

May you fumble with your keys
while trying to impress your boss.

May you dance naked on the photocopier
at the office Christmas party.

May you mistake
the drinks vending machine
for the fax machine
and fax your boss
three hot chocolates,
a black coffee
and a lemon squash.

May you accidentally
get your skirt caught
on the office printer and reveal
your Friday pants on a Tuesday.

May your boss turn into
Bruce Willis in character
as John McClane
at the monthly
staff debrief meeting.

May you set up your
own business selling
used jacket potatoes
and wonder
why nobody will offer
you a business loan.

May you accidentally order
a 'hot poo croissant' at the office
tea trolley for three days running.

May twenty-five shady deals pass
your consciousness during
a church outing to Southend-on-Sea.

Shopping

May you meet your friends at the mall wearing
an Elton John mask and be horrified when
seeing your image in a group photo.

May you be charged with
'squeezing and dislocating'
a yellow pepper
at the greengrocer's.

May you become totally devoid of taste
when shopping with your new boyfriend.

May your shopping trolley run into
the oat cereal at the supermarket.

May your head turn silver in
the Boxing Day sales.

May you forget
the dark-chocolate
rich tea biscuits
when you next go shopping.

May you discover you have bought
a year's supply of pizza base mix
at the checkout in Budgen.

May you feel like a mushroom
vol-au-vent at an auction.

May the store security

of your local supermarket

be convinced that you

did a huge poo in aisle six,

even though the event

never happened.

May you wonder why

you can't find

some of your shoes

and then discover

that your husband has

sold them all on eBay.

May you pronounce the word

'Lego' wrongly

when purchasing some

for your nephew.

Special Occasions

May your granddad wear his worst
brown trousers with cigarette burns
at your engagement party.

May your nostrils fill with
butterscotch blancmange
whilst giving a best man's speech.

May the vicar drop your niece
into the christening font.

May you get absolutely no
Facebook posts
from any of your friends
on your next birthday.

May your aunty send you
a flatworm kit for Christmas.

May you accidentally wedge

three sliver-plated goblets

between your two front teeth

at your son's wedding meal.

May your husband turn

into Goldie Hawn

on your wedding anniversary.

May you 'accidentally on purpose'

set off the fire alarm at

your daughter's graduation ceremony,

and then later shout 'Slag!'

as she goes on stage

to receive her certificate.

May the vicar catch you red-handed
substituting a baby potato
with a smiley face, drawn on with a felt tip, for
the Baby Jesus in the Nativity scene
at the front of the church.

The Theatre

May your uncle sit with his feet on
the shoulders of the person in front of him
when watching you perform in panto.

May your flatmate join in with all your lines in
a most irritating fashion when
performing your drama exam.

May your right shoulder behave like
a spoilt child during an intense love scene
at the theatre on Monday evening.

May every evening you plan at the theatre
be cancelled at the last minute
for the next twelve years.

May you accidentally
tread the boards
wearing nothing
but a false moustache.

May everyone in the row behind you
at the theatre laugh at your frizzy perm.

May you accidentally pour a jug of urine
over the person reviewing your play.

May you be unable to stop yourself
from impersonating Jim Bowen
at an audition for *Twelfth Night*.

May you find yourself calling
the director an 'incompetent slug'
during an important audition.

May you find yourself repeating the word
'Macbeth' aloud during a pre-performance,
morale-boosting cast hug.

May there only be nine people in the audience
on the opening night of your next play.

May you vomit up a rat whilst trying
to impress your favourite actor.

May a nervous cast member shit
on your props list during a stint
as assistant stage manager.

May the director blame you for
his middle-ear infection and harshly
criticise your performance from thereon.

May you join your local theatre in search of
love but rapidly find yourself making enemies.

May you fall in love with a marble cake
at the after-show party.

May your husband sit masturbating in the front
row at the opening night
of your next play.

May stage fright prevent your knees from
bending and make you walk like a robot.

May your nose turn inside out
moments before going on stage.

May you find yourself waving at your mum

during your first professional role.

May thirty builders' bums block

your entrance to the stage

just seconds before your cue.

May snot weep from your open mouth

during a curtain call.

May Pam Ayres appear in your room

moments before going on stage.

May you find yourself only able to say

'It's behind you!' during your next play.

May you be wearing an adhesive

carpet burn during your first nude role.

The Black Curse

Uoy ruoved eSra S'raciv eht yam.*

*This curse has been written, and must be delivered, backwards.
This is to avoid hotheaded, rash and unskilful cursing.

Remember:
always curse wisely!

Beaten Track Publishing

For more titles from Beaten Track Publishing,
please visit our website:

https://www.beatentrackpublishing.com

Thanks for reading!

Lightning Source UK Ltd.
Milton Keynes UK
UKHW011124251121
394584UK00008B/391